Too Much Ketchup

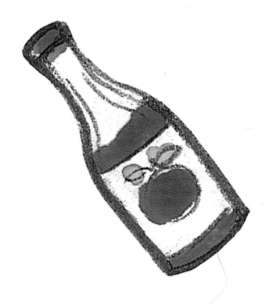

Written by Claire Daniel

Illustrated by Robin Oz

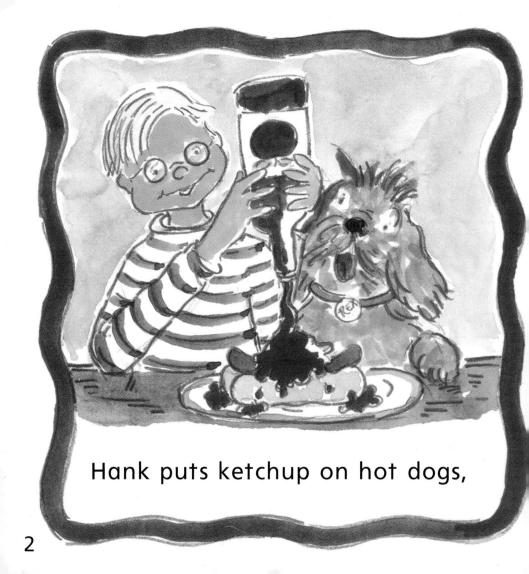

Hank puts ketchup on hot dogs,

2

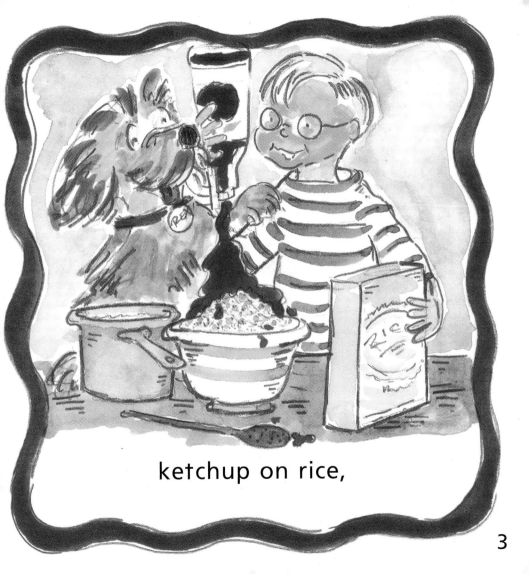

ketchup on rice,

3

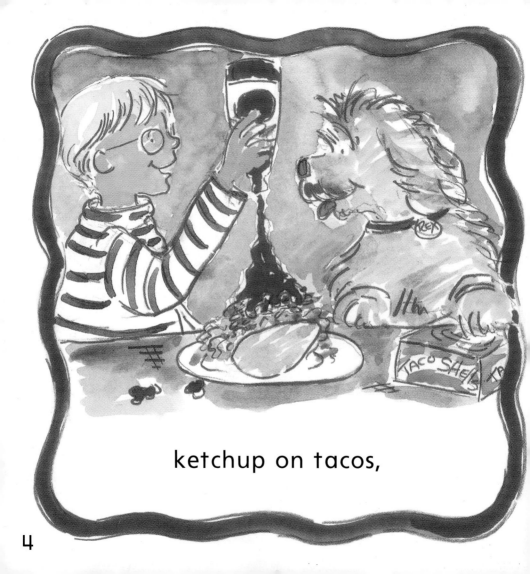

ketchup on tacos,

4

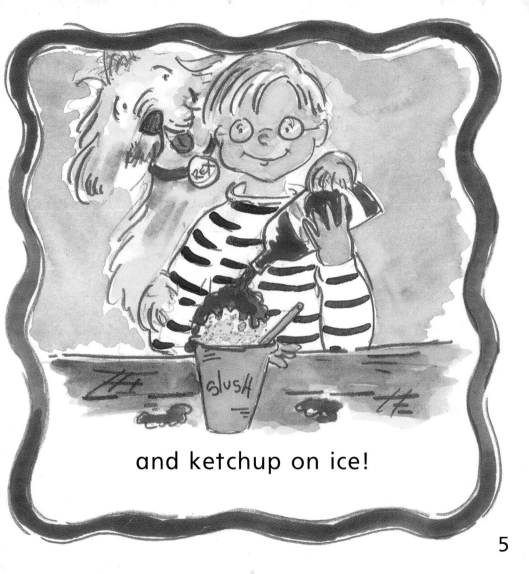

and ketchup on ice!

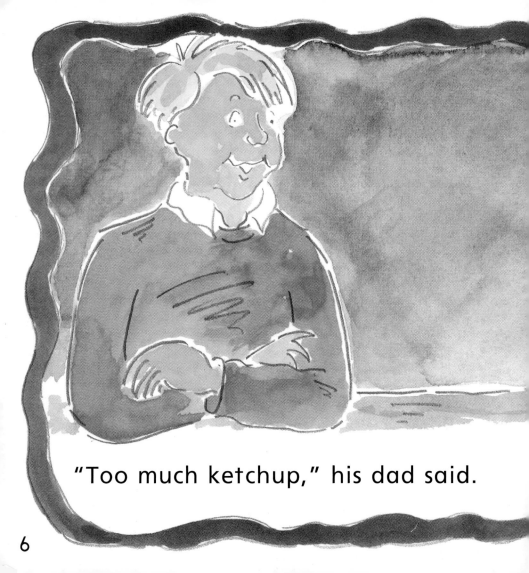

"Too much ketchup," his dad said.

6

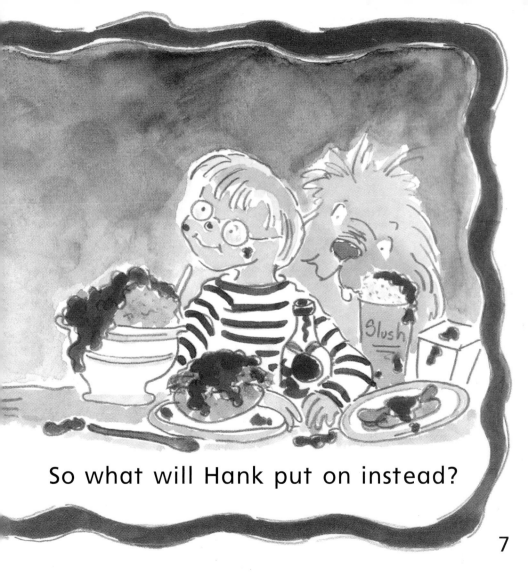

So what will Hank put on instead?

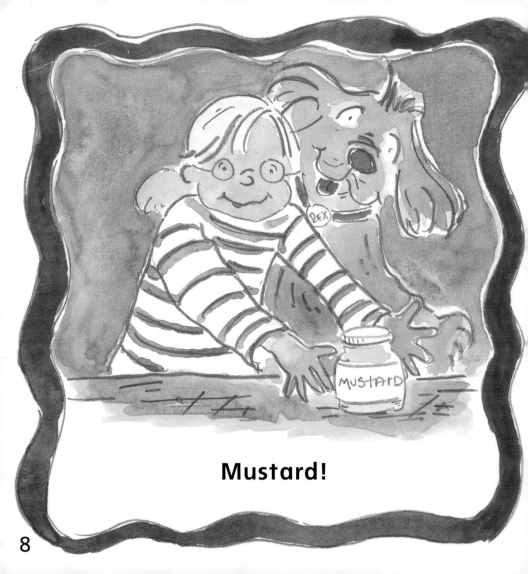

Mustard!

8